3 8002 01400 8223

KU-558-521

COVENTRY LIBRARIES

**Please return this book on or before
the last date stamped below.** 2006

PS130553 Disk 4

2006   CENTRAL LIBRARY

1 1 JUL 2007

2 3 DEC 2007
NII

To renew this book take it to any of
the City Libraries before
the date due for return

Coventry City Council

784·306

15 timeless classics

LIZA MINNELLI

Piano/vocal arrangements with guitar chord boxes

International Music Publications Ltd.

Arrangements and engraving by Artemis Music Limited
(www.artemismusic.com)
Photograph: Nicky J. Sims/Redferns Picture Library

Published 2005

© *International Music Publications Limited*
Griffin House 161 Hammersmith Road London England W6 8BS

Reproducing this music in any form is illegal and forbidden by the
Copyright, Designs and Patents Act, 1988.

CONTENTS

And All That Jazz

Words by John Kander
Music by Fred Ebb

© 1973 Kander-Ebb Inc, USA
Warner/Chappell Music Ltd, London W6 8BS

But The World Goes 'Round

Words by Fred Ebb
Music by John Kander

© 1977 EMI Catalogue Partnership, EMI Unart Catalog Inc and EMI United Partnership Ltd, USA
Worldwide print rights controlled by Warner Bros. Publications Inc/IMP Ltd

14

Bye Bye Blackbird

Words by Mort Dixon
Music by Ray Henderson

Pack up all my care and woe, here I go, sing-ing low, bye

© 1926 (renewed) Remick Music Corp, USA
Redwood Music Ltd, London NW1 8BD (for British Reversionary Territories)
Warner/Chappell North America Ltd, London W6 8BS (for World excl. British Reversionary Territories)

Make my bed and light the light, I'll be home late to-night. Black - bird.

Cabaret

Words by Fred Ebb
Music by John Kander

© 1966 Times Square Music Publications, USA
Carlin Music Corp, London NW1 8BD

1.

Eb   Fm⁷   Bb⁹

- ret._____

2.

Eb   Abm

- ret.   Come taste the wine,

Eb   Cm   Cm(maj⁷)   Cm⁷   F⁹

come hear the band,   come blow the horn, start   cel - e - brat - ing,

Bb⁷   Eb   Bb⁹   Bb⁹(♯5)   Eb   Bb⁷(♯5)

right this way, your ta - ble's wait - ing. 1. No use per - mit - ting some pro - phet of doom__
                                                        2. Start by ad - mit - ting from cra - dle to tomb__

Eb   Ebmaj⁷   Bbm⁷   Eb⁷

_____ to wipe ev - 'ry smile a - way;_____
_____ is - n't that long a stay;_____

City Lights

Words by John Kander
Music by Fred Ebb

The lit-tle old la - dy sat on the porch of the farm - house. The
lit-tle old la - dy rocked back and forth and_ cro - cheted._ Oh

© 1974 Kander-Ebb Inc, USA
Warner/Chappell Music Ltd, London W6 8BS

36

It Was A Good Time

(A.K.A. Rosy's Theme)

Words by Mack David and Mike Curb
Music by Maurice Jarre

© 1970 EMI Catalogue Partnership, EMI Feist Catalog Inc and EMI United Partnership Ltd, USA
Worldwide print rights controlled by Warner Bros. Publications Inc/IMP Ltd

42

_and we be-lieved that it would last for - ev - er.

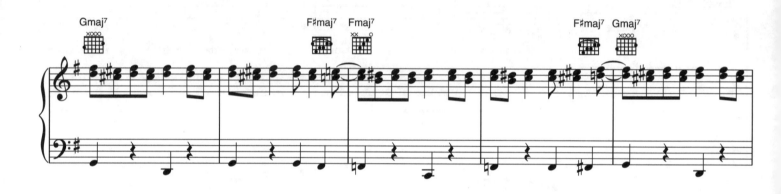

_and we be-lieved that it would last for - ev - er.

46

I Gotcha

Words and Music by Joe Tex

© 1971 Fort Knox Music Co and Trio Music Inc, USA
Sony/ATV Music Publishing (UK) Ltd, London W1F 7LP

50

Maybe This Time

Words by Fred Ebb
Music by John Kander

© 1963 Sunbeam-Music Inc, USA
Carlin Music Corp, London NW1 8BD

Money, Money

Words by Fred Ebb
Music by John Kander

Moderately bright

Mon - ey makes the world go a-round, the world go a-round, the world go a-round,

mon - ey makes the world go a-round, it makes the world go round.

© 1972 Alley Music Corp and Trio Music Co Inc, USA
Carlin Music Corp, London NW1 8BD

Mon - ey, mon - ey, mon - ey,   mon - ey, mon - ey, mon - ey,   mon - ey, mon - ey, mon - ey,

Ring Them Bells

Words by Fred Ebb
Music by John Kander

© 1972 Sunbeam-Music Inc, USA
Carlin Music Corp, London NW1 8BD

1. C⁷

2. C⁷

3. C⁷

Norm Sap -er - stein.' 5. She said, 'Are Twen -ty-nine F.__ 6. Yes, she was still be a - lone.__

D⁷ Am⁷ D⁷ G **Slow 4 beat**

7. Well, there's a mor - al to learn__ from lit - tle Shir - ley De - vore__ who had to

accel. poco a poco

D⁷

bor - row a thou__ to find a lov - er next door.__ You girls who live in a - part - ments, don't you

Em⁷ A⁷ D⁷ Eb⁷

rit.

stare at the wall,__ o - pen up the door and hur - ry out in the hall.__ And

Say Liza (Liza With a "Z")

Words by Fred Ebb
Music by John Kander

© 1972 Sunbeam-Music Inc, USA
Carlin Music Corp, London NW1 8BD

Some People

Words by Stephen Sondheim
Music by Jule Styne

© 1973 Norbeth Productions Inc and Chappell & Co Inc, USA
Warner/Chappell North America Ltd, London W6 8BS

81

Theme From New York, New York

Words by Fred Ebb
Music by John Kander

Moderately, with rhythm

Start spread-in' the news,   I'm leav-ing to-day,

I wan-na be a part_ of it   New York, New York.

© 1977 EMI Catalogue Partnership, EMI Unart Catalog Inc and EMI United Partnership Ltd, USA
Worldwide print rights controlled by Warner Bros. Publications Inc/IMP Ltd

Willkommen

Words by Fred Ebb
Music by John Kander

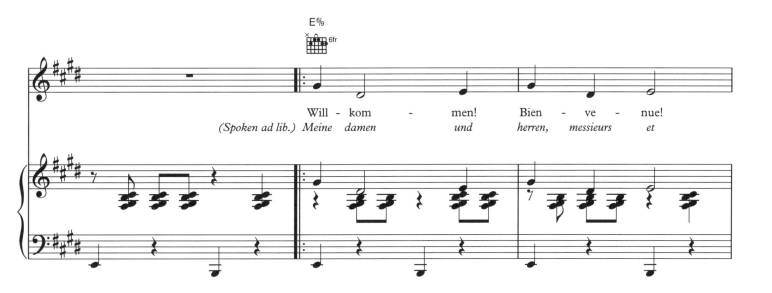

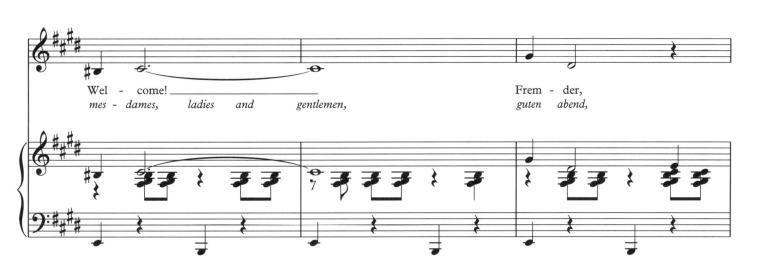

© 1966 Times Square Music Publications, USA
Carlin Music Corp, London NW1 8BD

Yes

Words by Fred Ebb
Music by John Kander

Moderato (with a lilt)

Yes. Say 'Yes'.

Life keeps hap-pen-ing ev-'ry day. Say 'Yes'. When

© 1971 Times Square Music Publications, USA
Carlin Music Corp, London NW1 8BD